A Healthy Pace

by Michael Scotto

illustrated by The Ink Circle

Tour de Midlandia
START

Once a year, the Midlandians held a bicycle race. It went through the mountains, through the forest, and over the rivers. The race was called the *Tour de Midlandia*.

Every year since the first race was held, Builda had won the *Tour*.

She loved to tell everyone about what a good rider she was. "I've broken every record in the books!" Builda declared.

Builda was quick about everything. She worked quickly, thought quickly, and even ate quickly. She expected everything around her to be quick, too.

"**There you are!**" Builda cried. She had been waiting all morning for Posta to arrive with her new bicycle parts. Posta delivered the mail in Midlandia.

"How can I keep on schedule if everyone else is so slow?" Builda asked.

"**I'm sorry,**" Posta told her. "I had a lot of stops to make along the way."

"I guess that you are just a **slow poke**, then," Builda said. "If I had your job, I'd be so quick that the mail would be delivered before it even got sent out!"

"I do not appreciate you teasing me!" Posta exclaimed.

"Then you'd better learn to ride like I can," Builda said. "After all, I am the best rider in all of Midlandia."

"You won't be able to brag after I beat you in the *Tour*," Posta grumbled. Oops! Posta had not meant to say that out loud.

"Beat me in the *Tour?*" Builda laughed. "That's the best joke I've heard all week!"

In that moment, Posta made a decision. "I am going to win the *Tour de Midlandia*," she declared.

But as she rode away, Posta began to worry. "Builda may brag a lot," Posta thought, "but she really is the quickest rider around. I'll need some help."

"**Thanks for helping me,** Coach," Posta said. Coach marched back and forth in front of her.

"We have a lot of work ahead of us, Posta," he said in his gruff voice. "But as long as you keep at it, getting in better shape is easy."

Coach rode in Posta's sidecar as she pedaled around Midlandia. "You need to be active at least an hour a day," Coach said. "That way, your heart and lungs will be **strong, strong, strong.**"

Coach and Posta did other exercises, too. **"Gallop like a horse!"** Coach said, and they galloped to make their legs strong.

"Do the kangaroo!" he said, and they hopped all the way across the playground.

"Slither like a snake!"
he said, and they slid to make
their bellies strong.

While Posta trained with Coach, Builda spent time at her bicycle factory. **"I don't need to practice,"** Builda thought. "I'm already quick enough. All that matters is that my bike is nice and shiny for the finish line."

After a week of training, Posta didn't feel **strong, strong, strong**. "I feel **tired, tired, tired**," she said.

"We've been working your muscles too hard," Coach said. "It's good to be strong, but there are other things to think about, too. So, I've brought you to meet my friend, **Sensei!**"

Sensei sat with Posta. "Builda is very fast," he said. "But the key to being healthy is not just being quick. You must be able to **keep a healthy pace.** Allow me to show you how."

Sensei taught Posta new ways to be healthy. First, they ate a snack together. "You should eat healthful foods," Sensei said. "When you are kind to your body, your body is kind to you."

Posta held her arms and legs out. "This seems a little weird," she told Sensei.

"It's good to do different kinds of stretches," he replied. "They help warm your muscles up and keep them from getting too tired."

Soon, it was race day. "I'm going to wear every one of my medals," Builda thought as she got dressed. "When Posta sees them, she'll really be nervous!"

Builda and Posta arrived at the starting line. While Builda showed off her bike and shiny medals, Posta thought about the things Coach and Sensei had taught her.

"Do not worry if Builda pulls ahead for a little while," they said. "Just keep a healthy pace."

At the starting line,
Coach blew his whistle.
The riders were off!

Builda pedaled in a burst until she pulled ahead of the pack. "These medals are heavier than I thought they'd be," she huffed, out of breath. Then, Builda saw one rider catching up in the distance.

It was Posta! **"Keep a healthy pace,"** Posta thought.

"I can't let Posta win!" Builda declared, and she pedaled off as hard as she could.

Builda kept ahead of Posta, but she could never get very far. Builda would pedal very quickly until she got tired and had to slow down. Then Posta would catch up. "Keep a healthy pace," Posta thought.

By the end of the day, the finish line was in sight. "I have...to ride...faster," Builda gasped. Posta was still right behind her! Builda pushed and pushed, but her muscles were too worn out. Posta breezed by her and crossed the finish line.

"And the winner is...Posta!"
Coach announced.

As Coach gave Posta her medal, Builda finally crossed the finish line. "I can't believe it!" she said, her medals all clanking together. **"You beat me!"**

"You tired yourself out showing off," Posta told Builda. "That's just not healthy. Like Coach and Sensei told me, **a healthy pace will win the race.**"

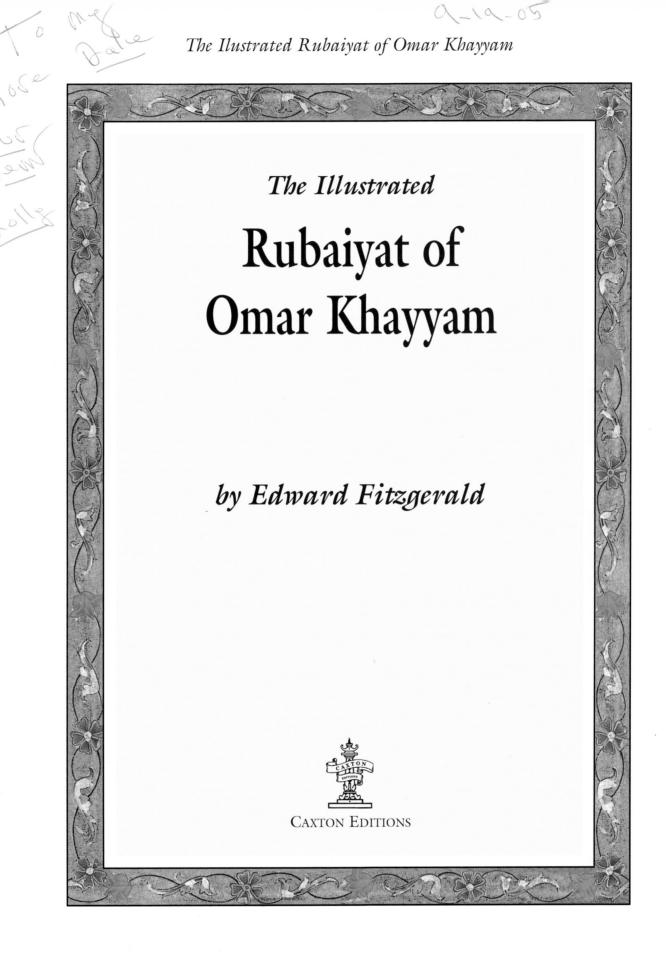

The Illustrated

Rubaiyat of Omar Khayyam

by Edward Fitzgerald

CAXTON EDITIONS

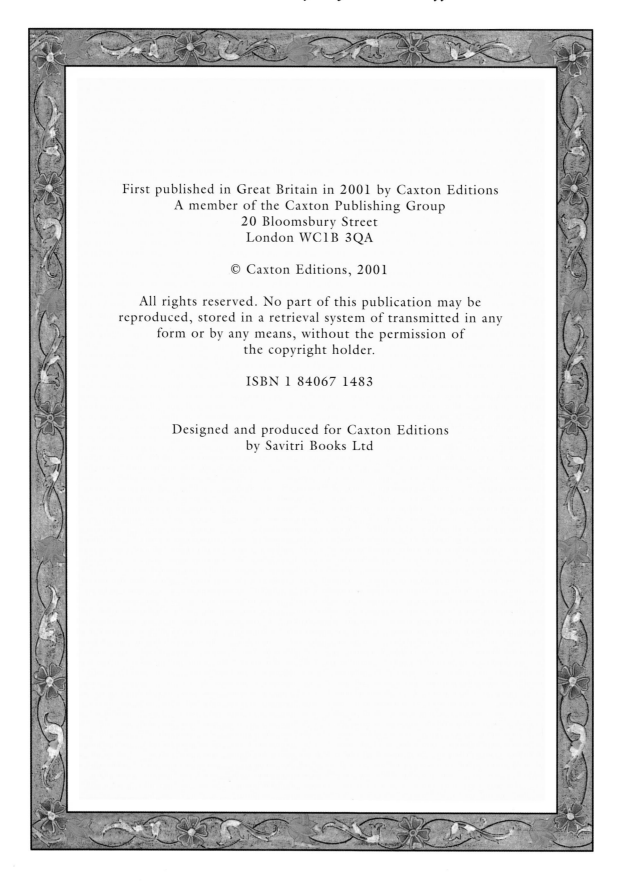

First published in Great Britain in 2001 by Caxton Editions
A member of the Caxton Publishing Group
20 Bloomsbury Street
London WC1B 3QA

ISBN 1 84067 1483

Designed and produced for Caxton Editions
by Savitri Books Ltd

INTRODUCTION

Omar Khayyam – the astronomer-poet of Persia – lived between c. 1050 and c. 1123. Until 1859, when Edward Fitzgerald carried out a free translation of the *Rubaiyat*, Omar Khayyam was chiefly known in the west as the mathematical genius who had reformed the Muslim calendar and whose work on algebra was translated by Woepke in 1851. But Fitzgerald's translation of part of his great poetic work was a revelation to the western world.

Whether through the sheer poetry of the text or its underlying Sufi mysticism, the *Rubaiyat* continues to delight modern audiences, just as much as it did the mid-nineteenth century reader. The present edition, richly illustrated with the paintings of the Indo-Persian artist, Muraqqa Chugtai, cannot fail to delight.

I

Awake! for Morning in the

Bowl of Night

Has flung the Stone that puts

the Stars to Flight:

And lo! the Hunter of

the East has caught

The Sultan's Turret in a

Noose of Light.

Left: Persian Idyll

II

Dreaming when Dawn's Left
   Hand was in the Sky, I heard a Voice
within the
   Tavern cry,
"Awake, my Little ones,
   and fill the Cup
Before Life's Liquor in its
   Cup be dry."

III

And as the Cock crew, those

who stood before

The Tavern shouted—"Open

then the Door !

You know how little while

we have to stay,

And once departed, may

return no more."

IV

Now the New year reviving

old Desires,

The thoughtful Soul to

Solitude retires,

Where the White Hand

Of Moses on the Bough

Puts out, and Jesus from the

Ground suspires.

Right: Dancing Stars

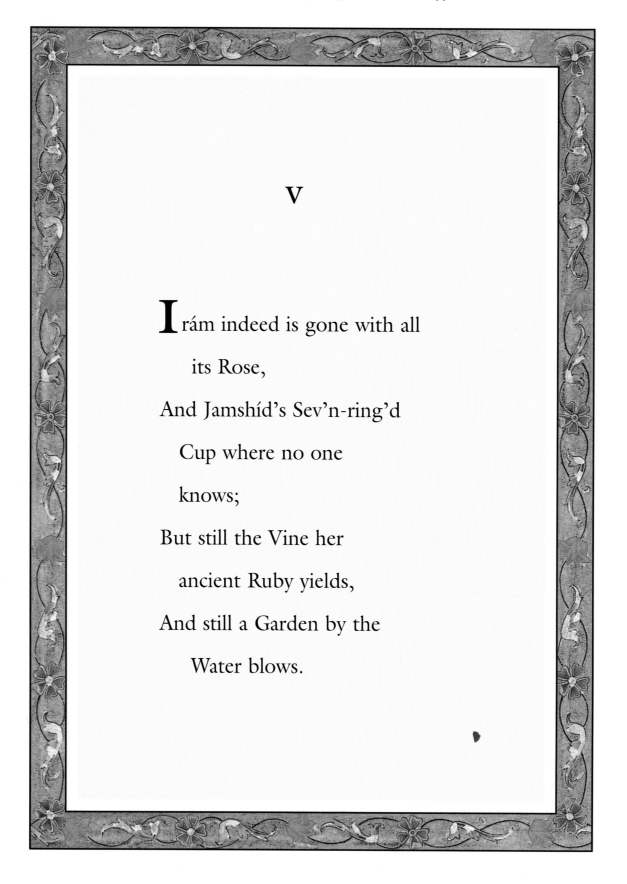

V

Irám indeed is gone with all

its Rose,

And Jamshíd's Sev'n-ring'd

Cup where no one

knows;

But still the Vine her

ancient Ruby yields,

And still a Garden by the

Water blows.

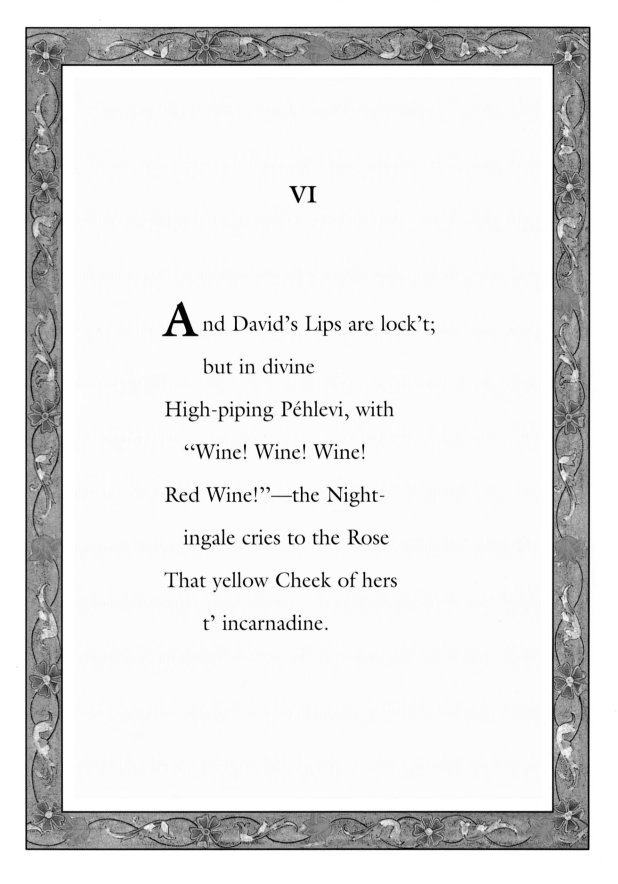

VI

And David's Lips are lock't;
but in divine
High-piping Péhlevi, with
"Wine! Wine! Wine!
Red Wine!"—the Night-
ingale cries to the Rose
That yellow Cheek of hers
t' incarnadine.

VII

Come, fill the Cup, and in the

Fire of Spring

The Winter Garment of

Repentance fling:

The Bird of Time has but

a little way

To fly—and Lo! the Bird is

on the Wing.

Right: The Brimming Cup

VIII

And look – a thousand
Blossoms
   with the Day
Woke – and a thousand scat-
   ter'd into Clay:
And this first Summer
   Month that brings the
   Rose
Shall take Jamshíd and
   Kaikobád away.

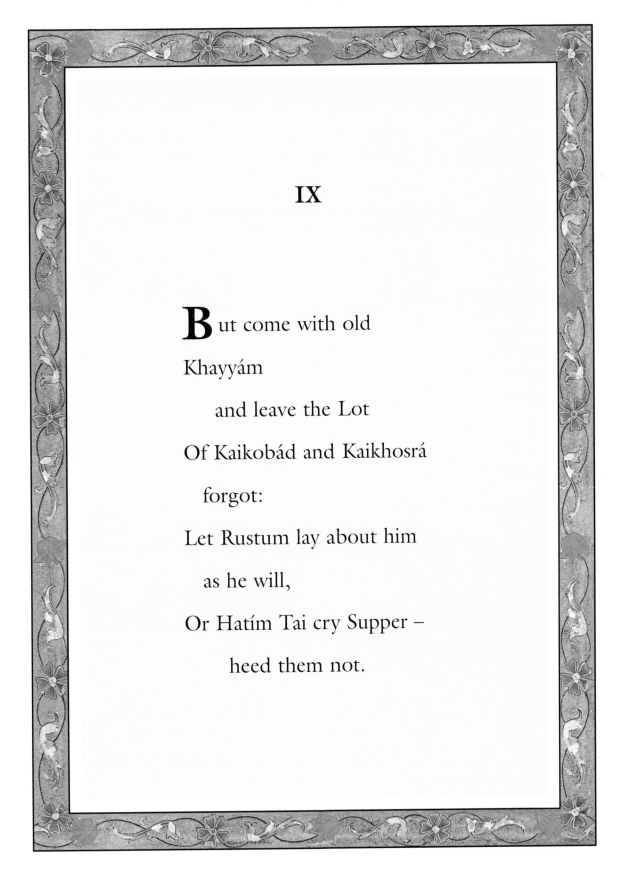

IX

But come with old

Khayyám

   and leave the Lot

Of Kaikobád and Kaikhosrá

   forgot:

Let Rustum lay about him

   as he will,

Or Hatím Tai cry Supper –

   heed them not.

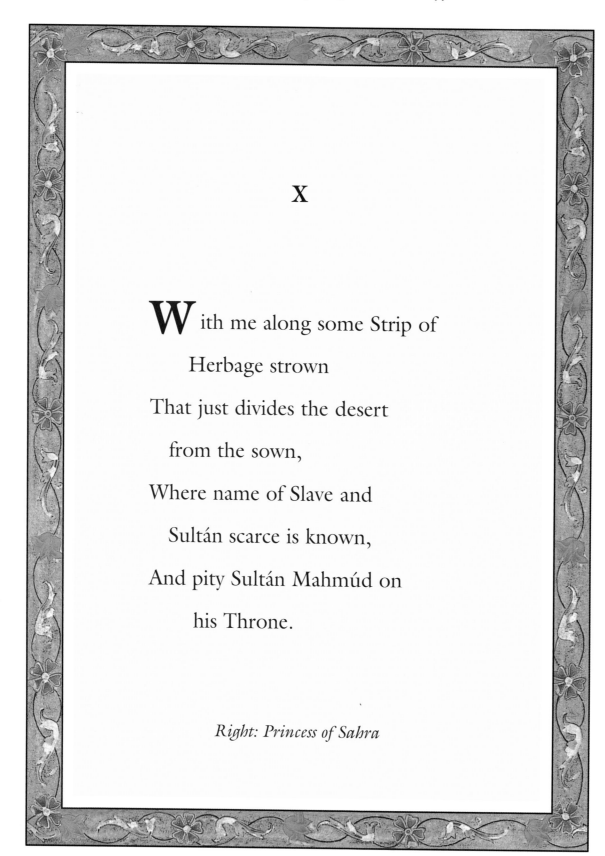

X

With me along some Strip of
Herbage strown
That just divides the desert
from the sown,
Where name of Slave and
Sultán scarce is known,
And pity Sultán Mahmúd on
his Throne.

Right: Princess of Sahra

XI

Here with a Loaf of Bread

beneath the Bough

A Flask of Wine, a Book of

Verse – and Thou

Beside me singing in the

Wilderness –

And Wilderness is Paradise

now.

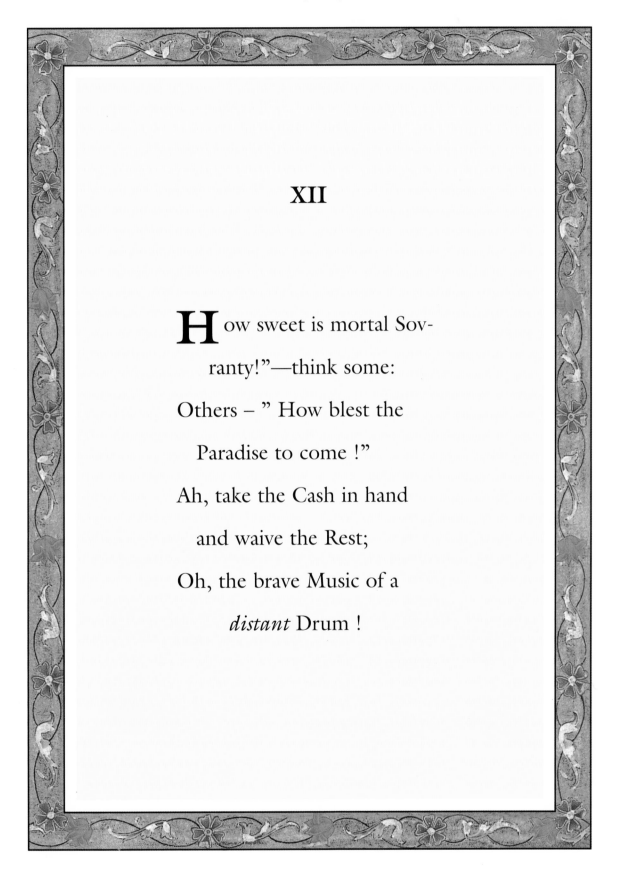

XII

"How sweet is mortal Sov-
ranty!"—think some:

Others – " How blest the

Paradise to come !"
Ah, take the Cash in hand

and waive the Rest;
Oh, the brave Music of a

distant Drum !

XIII

Look to the Rose that blows

about us – "Lo,

Laughing," she says, "into

the World I blow:

At once the silken Tassel

of my Purse

Tear, and its Treasure on the

Garden throw."

Left: The Poet's Vision

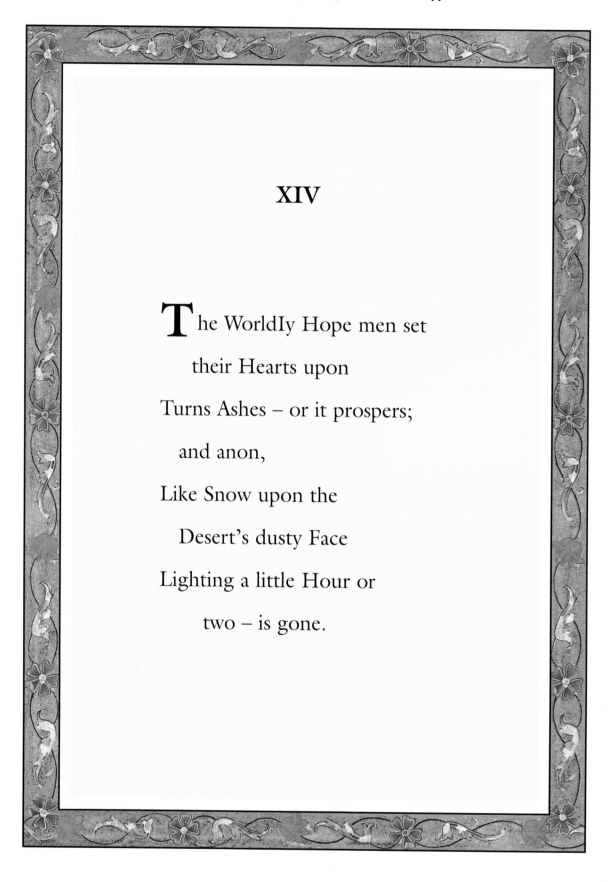

XIV

The WorldIy Hope men set

their Hearts upon

Turns Ashes – or it prospers;

and anon,

Like Snow upon the

Desert's dusty Face

Lighting a little Hour or

two – is gone.

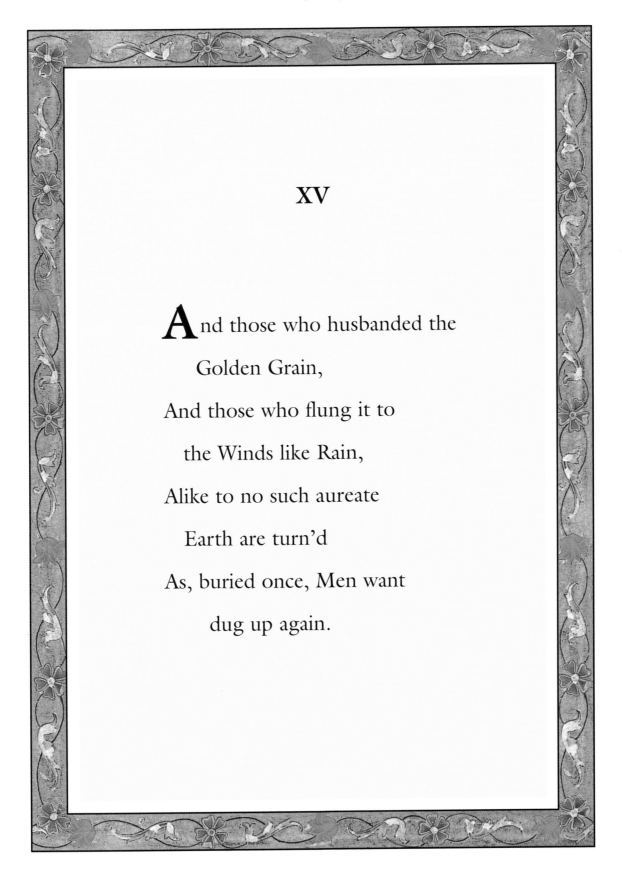

XV

And those who husbanded the

Golden Grain,

And those who flung it to

the Winds like Rain,

Alike to no such aureate

Earth are turn'd

As, buried once, Men want

dug up again.

XVI

Think, in this battered Cara-

vanserai

Whose Doorways are alter-

nate Night and Day,

How Sultán after Sultán

with his Pomp

Abode his Hour or two, and

went his way.

Right: The Web of Life

XVII

They say the Lion and the

Lizard keep

The Courts where Jamshíd

gloried and drank deep:

And Bahrám, that great

Hunter – the Wild Ass

Stamps o'er his Head, and he

lies fast asleep.

Left: The Land of Fragrance

XVIII

I sometimes think that never

blows so red

The Rose as where some

buried Caesar bled

That every Hyacinth the

Garden wears

Dropt in its Lap from some

once lovely Head.

Right: The Carpet Girl

XIX

And this delightfuI Herb whose
tender Green
Fledges the River's Lip on
which we lean –
Ah, lean upon it lightly!
for who knows
From what once Lovely Lip
it springs unseen!

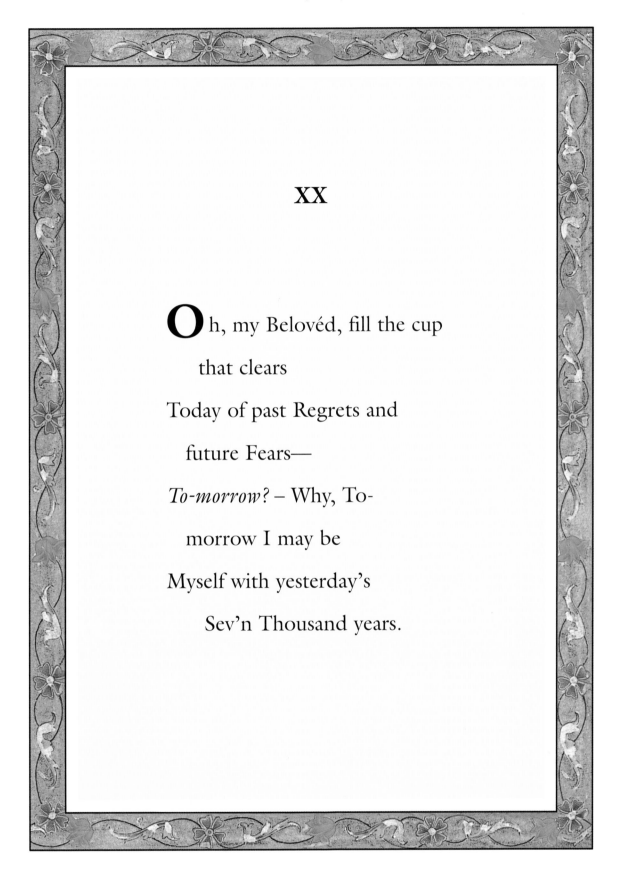

XX

Oh, my Belovéd, fill the cup
that clears

Today of past Regrets and
future Fears—

To-morrow? – Why, To-
morrow I may be

Myself with yesterday's
Sev'n Thousand years.

XXI

Lo! some we loved, the love-

liest and the best

That Time and Fate of all

their Vintage prest,

Have drunk their Cup a

Round or two before,

And one by one crept silently

to Rest.

Right: Reflections

XXII

And we, that now make merry

in the Room

They left, and Summer dresses

in new Bloom,

Ourselves must we beneath

the Couch of Earth

Descend, ourselves to make

a Couch—for whom?

XXIII

Ah, make the most of what we
   yet may spend,
Before we too into the Dust
   descend;
Dust into Dust, and under
   Dust, to lie,
Sans Wine, sans Song, sans
   Singer, and – sans End!

XXIV

Like for those who for To-day

  prepare,

And those that after a To-

  morrow stare,

A Muezzín from the Tower

  of Darkness cries,

"Fools! your Reward is

  neither Here nor There!"

Right: The Old Lamp

XXV

Why, all the Saints and Sages

who discuss'd

Of the Two Worlds so

learnedly, are thrust

Like foolish Prophets forth

their Words to Scorn

Are scatter'd, and their

Mouths are stopt with

Dust.

XXVI

Oh, come with old Khayyám,
  and leave the Wise
    To talk; one thing is certain,
      that Life flies;
One thing is certain, and
  the Rest is Lies;
The Flower that once has
  blown for ever dies.

XXVII

Myself when young did eagerly

frequent

Doctor and Saint, and heard

great Argument

About it and about, but

evermore

Came out by the same Door

as in I went.

Right: The Tutor

XXVIII

With them the Seed of Wisdom

did I sow,

And with my own hand

Labour'd it to grow:

And this was all the

Harvest that I reap'd –

"I came like Water, and like

Wind I go."

XXIX

Into this Universe, and *why*

not knowing,

Nor *whence*, like Water

willy-nilly flowing!

And out of it, as Wind

along the Waste,

I know not *whither*, willy-

nilly blowing.

XXX

What, without asking, hither hurried *whence?*
And, without asking, *whither* hurried hence!
Another and another Cup to drown
The memory of this Imperti-
nence!

Right: Soliloquy

XXXl

Up from Earth's Centre through
the Seventh Gate

I rose, and on the Throne of
Saturn sate,

And many Knots unravel'd
by the Road;

But not the Knot of Human
Death and Fate.

XXXII

There was a Door to which I

found no Key:

There was a Veil past which

I could not see:

Some little Talk awhile of

Me and Thee

There seemed– and then no

more of Thee and Me.

XXXIII

Then to the rolling Heav'n
itself I cried,

Asking, "What Lamp had
Destiny to guide

Her little Children stumbling
in the Dark?"

And –"A blind understand-
ing!" Heaven replied.

Right: The Captive Bird

XXXIV

Then to the earthen Bowl did

    I adjourn

My Lip the secret Well of

    Life to learn:

And Lip to Lip it murmur'd

    –" While you live

Drink! – for once dead you

    never shall return."

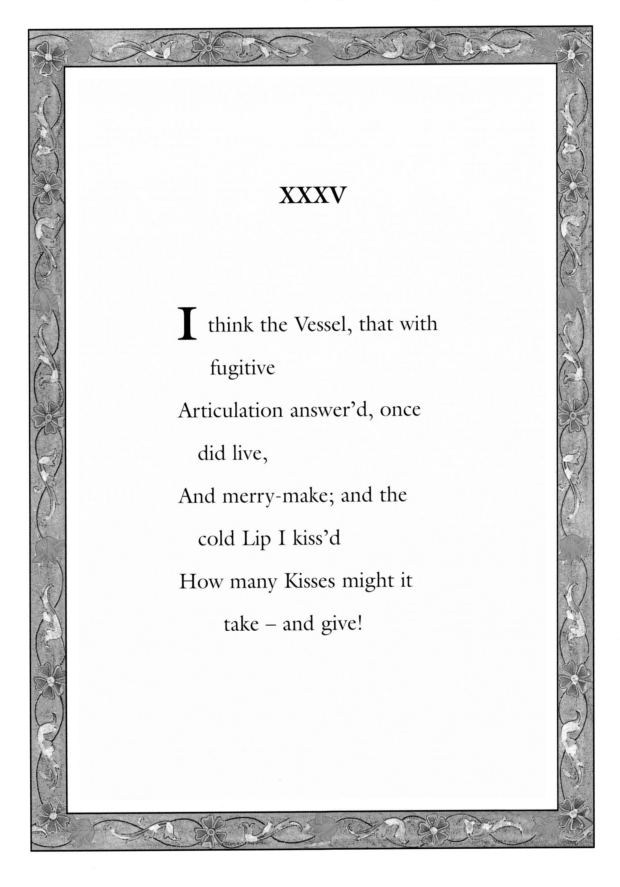

XXXV

I think the Vessel, that with
fugitive
Articulation answer'd, once
did live,
And merry-make; and the
cold Lip I kiss'd
How many Kisses might it
take – and give!

XXXVI

For in the Market-place, one
Dusk of day,

I watch'd the Potter thumping
his wet Clay:

And with its all obliterated
Tongue

It murmur'd – "Gently,
Brother, gently, pray!"

Right: The Extinguished Flame

XXXVII

O h, fill the Cup: – what boots

    it to repeat

How time is slipping under-

    neath our Feet:

Unborn To-morrow and

    dead Yesterday,

Why fret about them if

    To-day be sweet!

XXXVIII

One Moment in Annihilation's

Waste,

One Moment, of the Well

of Life to taste, –

The Stars are setting and

the Caravan

Starts for the Dawn of

Nothing – Oh, make

haste!

XXXIX

How long, how long, in infinite

  Pursuit

Of This and That endeavour

  and dispute?

Better be merry with the

  fruitful Grape

Than sadden after none, or

  bitter, Fruit.

Right: The Song Offering

XL

Y ou know, my Friends, how

long since in my House

For a new Marriage I did

make Carouse:

Divorced old barren

Reason from my Bed,

And took the Daughter of

the Vine to Spouse.

XLI

F or "Is" and "Is-not" though

with Rule and Line,

And "Up-and-down" *with-*

out, I could define,

I yet in all I only cared to

know,

Was never deep in anything

but—Wine.

XLII

And lately, by the Tavern

Door agape,

Came stealing through the

Dusk an Angel Shape

Bearing a Vessel on his

Shoulder; and

He bid me taste of it; and

'twas – the Grape!

Right: The Saki

XLIII

The Grape that can with Logic

absolute

The Two-and-Seventy jarring

Sects confute:

The subtle Alchemist that

in a Trice

Life's leaden Metal into Gold

transmute.

XLIV

The mighty Mahmúd, the victorious Lord

That all the misbelieving and

black Horde

Of Fears and Sorrows

that infest the Soul

Scatters and slays with his

enchanted Sword.

XLV

But leave the Wise to

wrangle,

   and with me

The Quarrel of the Universe

   let be:

And, in some corner of the

   Hubbub coucht,

Make Game of that which

   makes as much of Thee.

Right: Flowers of Yesterday

XLVI

For in and out, above, about,
below,

"Tis nothing but a Magic
Shadow-show,

Play'd in a Box whose
Candle is the Sun,

Round which we Phantom
Figures come and go.

XLVII

And if the Wine you drink, the

    Lip you press,

End in the Nothing all Things

    end in – yes –

Then fancy while Thou

    art, Thou art but what

Thou shalt be – Nothing

    Thou shalt not be less.

XLVIII

While the Rose blows along the

River Brink,

With old Khayyám the Ruby

Vintage drink:

And when the Angel with

his darker Draught

Draws up to Thee – take that,

and do not shrink.

Right: Desert in Bloom

XLIX

Tis all a Chequer-board of

Nights and Days

Where Destiny with Men

for Pieces plays:

Hither and thither moves,

and mates, and slays,

And one by one back in the

Closet lays.

L

The Ball no Question makes

   of Ayes and Noes,

But Right or Left as strikes

   the Player goes;

And He that toss'd Thee

   down into the Field,

He knows about it all– He

   knows – He knows!

LI

The Moving Finger writes:

and, having writ,

Moves on: nor all thy Piety

nor Wit

Shall lure it back to cancel

half a Line,

Nor all thy Tears wash out

a Word of it.

Right:Observation

LII

And that inverted BowI we call
The Sky,
Whereunder crawling coop't
we live and die,
Lift not thy hands to *It* for
heIp – for It
Rolls impotently on as Thou
or I.

LIII

With Earth's first Clay They
did the last Man's knead,
And then of the Last
    Harvest sow'd the Seed:
Yea, the first Morning of
    Creation wrote
What the Last Dawn of
    Reckoning shall read.

LIV

I tell Thee this – When, starting

from the Goal,

Over the shoulders of the

flaming Foal

Of Heav'n Parwin and

Mushtara they flung,

In my predestin'd Plot of

Dust and Soul.

Right: Serenade

LV

The Vine had struck a Fibre;

which about

If clings my Being – let the

Súfi flout;

Of my Base Metal may

be filed a Key,

That shall unlock the Door

he howls without.

LVI

And this I know: whether the

one True Light,

Kindle to Love, or Wrath

consume me quite,

One Glimpse of It within

the Tavern caught

Better than in the Temple

lost outright.

LVII

Oh Thou, who didst with
Pitfall and with Gin
Beset the Road I was to
wander in,
Thou wilt not with Pre-
destination round
Enmesh me, and impute my
Fall to Sin?

Right: The Wasted Vigil

LVIII

Oh Thou, who Man of baser

Earth didst make

And who with Eden didst

devise the Snake;

For all the Sin wherewith

the Face of man

Is blacken'd, Man's Forgive-

ness give – and take!

LIX

Listen again. One Evening
at the Close
Of Ramazán, ere the better
Moon arose,
In that old Potter's Shop
I stood alone
With the clay Population
round in Rows.

LX

And, strange to tell, among that

    Earthen Lot

Some could articulate, while

    others not:

And suddenly one more

    impatient cried –

"Who *is* the Potter, pray, and

    who the Pot?"

Right: The Id Moon

LXI

T hen said another – "Surely not
   in vain

"My substance from the common Earth was ta'en;

That He who subtly

   wrought me into Shape

Should stamp me back to

   common Earth again."

LXII

Another said "Why, ne'er a

peevish Boy

Would break the Bowl from

which he drank in Joy;

Shall He that *made* the

Vessel in pure Love

And Fancy, in an after Rage

destroy !"

LXIII

One answered this; but after

Silence spake

A Vessel of a more ungainly

Make:

"They sneer at me for

leaning all awry;

What! did the Hand then of

the Potter shake?"

Left: The Resting Place

LXIV

Said one – "FoIks of a surly

    Tapster tell,

And daub his visage with the

    Smoke of HelI;

They talk of some strict

    Testing of us – Pish!

He's a Good Fellow and

    'twill all be well."

LXV

Then said another with a long-
drawn Sigh,

"My Clay with long Oblivion
is gone dry:

But, fill me with the old
familiar Juice,

Methinks I might recover by-
and-bye! "

LXVI

So while the Vessels one by
one were speaking,

One spied the little Crescent
all were seeking:

And then they jogged each
other, "Brother! Brother!

Hark to the Porter's Shoulder-
knot a-creaking!"

right: The Flower Gatherers

LXVII

Oh, with the Grape my fading

Life provide,

And wash my Body whence

the Life has died,

And in a Winding-sheet

of Vine-leaf wrapt,

So bury me by some sweet

Garden side.

LXVIII

That ev'n my buried Ashes

such a Snare

Of Perfume shall Ring up into

the Air,

As not a True Believer

passing by

But shall be overtaken un-

aware.

LXIX

I ndeed the Idols I have loved

so long

Have done my Credit in

Men's Eye much Wrong,

Have drowned my Honour

in a shaIIow Cup,

And soId my Reputation for

a Song.

Right: The Music Lesson

LXX

I ndeed, indeed, Repentance oft
  before

I swore – but was I sober
  when I swore?

And then and then came
  Spring, and Rose-in-hand,

My thread-bare Penitence
  a-pieces tore.

LXXI

And much as Wine has played
the Infidel,
And robb'd me of my Robe
of Honour – well,
I often wonder what the
Vintners buy
One half so precious as the
Goods they sell.

LXXII

Alas, that Spring should vanish

with the Rose!

That youth's sweet-scented

Manuscript should close!

The NightingaIe that in the

Branches sang,

Ah, whence, and whither flown

again, who knows?

Above: The Song of Life

LXXIII

Ah, Love! could thou and I

with Fate conspire

To grasp this sorry Scheme

of Things entire,

Would not we shatter it

to bits and then

Re-mould it nearer to the

Heart's Desire!

LXXIV

Ah, Moon of my Delight who

know'st no Wane,

The Moon of Heaven is

rising once again:

How oft hereafter rising

shall she look

Through this same Garden

after me – in vain!

LXXV

And when Thyself with shining

Foot shall pass

Among the Guests Star-

scattered on the Grass

And in thy joyous Errand

reach the Spot

Where I made one – turn

down an empty Glass!

TAMÁM SHUD

Right: Where the Way Ends